Deserts

Joy Palmer

Watts Books
London • New York • Sydney

© Watts Books 1991
Paperback edition 1995

Watts Books
96 Leonard Street
London EC2A 4RH

Franklin Watts Australia
14 Mars Road
Lane Cove
NSW 2066

ISBN: 0 7496 0573 1 (hardback)
ISBN: 0 7496 2321 7 (paperback)

10 9 8 7 6 5 4 3 2 1

Editor: Ambreen Husain
Designer: Shaun Barlow
Cover Design: K and Co
Artwork: Hayward Art Group

Educational Advisor: Joy Richardson
Consultant: Miranda MacQuitty

A CIP catalogue record for this book
is available from the British Library

Printed in Italy
by G. Canale & Co. SpA

Contents

What are deserts?

Deserts are places where very little rain falls. Because the weather is nearly always dry, very few plants can grow there. Many deserts are very hot places during the day, but are cold during the night. Other deserts are cold for most of the year. Animals and plants, as well as some people, have found ways to live in dry desert areas.

▽ The sands of the Sahara, the world's largest desert.

Where are deserts?

Deserts are found in areas where dry winds blow across the land. These can be a long way from the sea, where moist sea winds do not reach. They can also be areas separated from the sea by high mountains. Many deserts are in **tropical** areas near the **equator**. The equator is an imaginary line around the middle of the earth.

▷ The Sonoran Desert in the United States is famous for its cactus plants.

The equator

Areas of desert

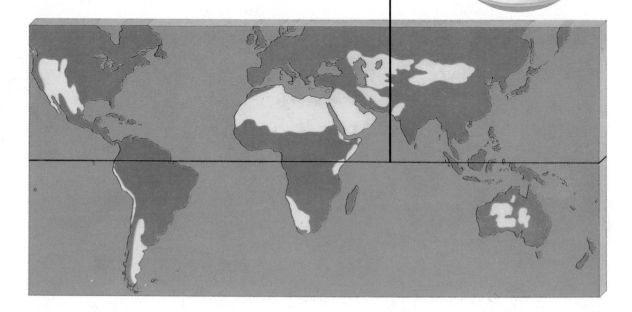

What are deserts like?

Deserts can be sandy, stony or rocky. In sandy deserts, strong winds can blow the sand into smooth hills called **dunes**. The wind can be very powerful. It blows sand and dust about, wearing away rocks and changing the shape of sand dunes. Many desert lands have more rocks and stones than sand. There are often steep cliffs and rocky mountains in these areas.

▷ Over hundreds of years, desert rocks are worn into amazing shapes by the sand and wind.

▽ Sand dunes are shaped by the strong desert winds.

What is the weather like?

All deserts are very dry places. Dry winds blow hot or cold air across the land. Some deserts are hot all year round. Others are cold during winter.

Sometimes there can be a huge rainstorm in a desert. The rainfall is so heavy that it splashes on to the ground with great force. Animals may drown and plants may be washed away in **floods**.

▷ Heavy rainfall can cause a temporary lake to form where a river has flooded.

▷ A small whirlwind, whipping up dust into the air, moves across the dry land.

Plants

Desert plants have special ways of surviving in a dry place with very little water. Cactus plants do this by soaking up water when the rain comes and storing it in their thick fleshy stems. Some desert plants have very long roots so that they can get water from deep underground. Many plant seeds lie in the desert ground for years. When it rains, they suddenly start to grow.

▷ After a rainstorm, flowering plants fill the desert with colour.

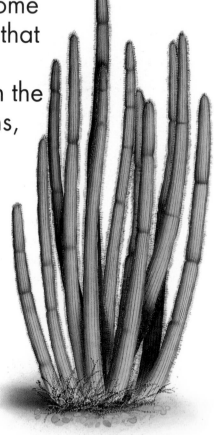

▷ This century plant produces just one flower in its lifetime.

◁ The Mexican poppy produces bright golden flowers after rain has fallen.

△ The organ-pipe cactus can store large amounts of water in its stems.

10

▽ All cactus plants
can produce
flowers. This is a
prickly pear cactus.

△ The welwitschia
is found only in the
Namib Desert in
Africa.

Mammals and birds

In hot deserts, most creatures come out at night when the desert cools down. During the day, they try to find shade from the sun. Many smaller animals dig burrows underground. They use them to shelter from the sun.

Many desert animals get some of the water they need by eating juicy plants. Desert birds also get water from the seeds and insects they eat.

▽ The elf owl nests in the stem of a large cactus, in a hole made by a desert woodpecker.

◁ The ground squirrel can use its large bushy tail as a sun umbrella.

▷ The road runner is a desert bird that spends most of its life on the ground.

▽ The gemsbok are antelopes that live in the deserts of southern Africa.

▽ The jerboa nests in burrows or under rocks during the heat of the day.

▷ The red kangaroo can keep itself cool by licking the fur on its arms.

△ The fennec fox has huge ears. They help it to get rid of its body heat and keep cool.

13

Camels

Camels are well built for life in the desert. They can drink 100 litres of water at a time, then survive for up to a whole week without another drink. There are two sorts of camels. A **dromedary** has one hump on its back. A **bactrian camel** has two humps. The humps on a camel's back contain fat which can be used as food on long journeys.

▽ Desert people use camels as a means of transport.

14

bactrian camel

dromedary

▽ A camel's foot has two toes joined by a pad. This acts like a web and helps stop the camel sinking into the sand as it walks.

△ Camels have bushy eyebrows and long thick eyelashes. These help keep sand out of their eyes.

Reptiles and minibeasts

There are many **reptiles**, such as snakes and lizards, in the desert. Lizards have tough scaly skins to protect them from the sun. Often they bury themselves in the sand to keep cool.

Minibeasts, such as scorpions, hunt for insects and other small animals in the sand.

▷ The sidewinder snake moves sideways across the sand.

△ This honeypot ant stores nectar in its body.

▽ The skink is a lizard that eats insects.

▷ This gecko has broad webbed feet to help it move quickly across the sand.

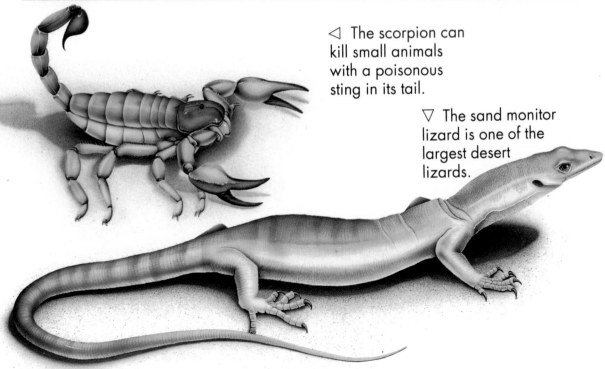

◁ The scorpion can
kill small animals
with a poisonous
sting in its tail.

▽ The sand monitor
lizard is one of the
largest desert
lizards.

People

It is not easy for people to survive in the desert. Food and water are very hard to find. But people in many parts of the world have adapted to living in the desert.

People of the desert live in groups or **tribes**. Many desert people are **nomads**, which means they move around from place to place. Others settle in one place and find ways of growing crops.

▷ Baluchi nomads set up camp wherever they find grazing land for their animals.

▽ The Tuareg people of the Sahara Desert are nomads.

△ The Bushman people live in the Kalahari Desert in Africa.

△ The Hopi Indians farm crops in the desert of the south-western United States.

How the people live

Desert nomads move from place to place in search of grazing land and water. They use camels or donkeys to carry their tents and other belongings. They keep animals such as goats and sheep.

Some desert people settle in places where water can always be found. They build houses and farm the land.

▷ Bedouin nomads in North Africa setting up camp.

▷ Inside a home of Bedouin nomads.

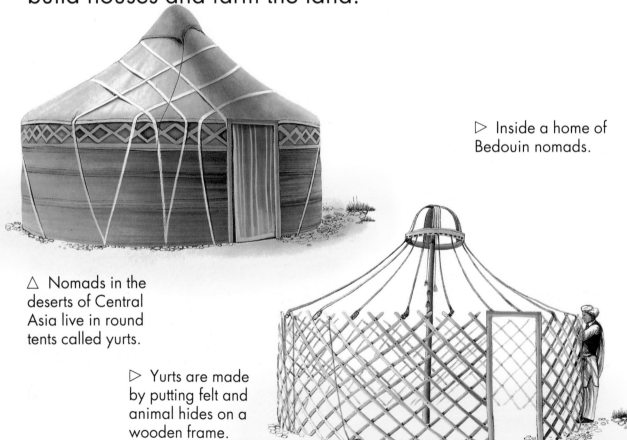

△ Nomads in the deserts of Central Asia live in round tents called yurts.

▷ Yurts are made by putting felt and animal hides on a wooden frame.

Life around an oasis

An **oasis** is a place in a desert where there is water throughout the year. Oasis water usually comes from underground streams or pools. Towns and villages are built around the oasis because there is a good supply of water. People can grow food crops such as date palms, olives and wheat.

▷ An oasis is like a green island in a sea of sand.

▽ Bricks made of mud and straw have been used to build these desert houses.

Ways of survival

Desert people have many ways of surviving. They know where water can be found underground. They also know which plants contain water.

Some desert houses are made of stone and dried earth. This keeps the inside of the house cool in the heat of the day. Many desert people wear long loose clothing to protect them from the heat and dust.

▷ The clothes of the Tuareg protect them from the sand, the wind and the hot sun.

◁ A Bushman digs out tubers. These are fleshy roots which can be squeezed for water.

Using the deserts

Many desert areas are being irrigated so that crops can be grown. Water from an oasis is carried through pipes and canals on to fields. This is called **irrigation**.

Some deserts have large underground supplies of oil or gas. In other deserts there are **minerals** such as gold and copper.

▽ Food plants such as wheat and millet are grown in irrigated fields.

◁ Oil drilling rigs in the desert. Many tests are made before starting a well.

The spreading desert

The desert areas of our world are growing in size. Large areas of fertile land close to deserts are becoming dry and bare. One reason for this is a change in our planet's **climate**. There have been many years of **drought** with very little rain. Trees and grasses on the desert edges have died. Overgrazing and bad farming methods leave the land bare.

▷ Desert sands have slowly taken over small villages.

▷ Years of drought leave the land dry and cracked.

Things to do

- Grow your own desert plants at home. Garden shops and nurseries sell seeds of cactus plants. Keep the cacti in a warm place. They do not need much water.

- Make your own sand dunes. Place some dry sand in a shallow tray. Blow gently at it through a drinking straw. You are making sand dunes, just as the wind does in sandy deserts.

Useful Addresses:

Survival International
310 Edgware Road
London
W2 1DY

SOS Sahel International UK
1 Tolpuddle Street
London
N1 0XT

Glossary

bactrian camel A camel with two humps, native to the cold deserts of Central Asia.

climate The weather conditions of an area over a period of years.

dromedary A camel with one hump, native to the deserts of Arabia and North Africa.

drought A long period with very little or no rainfall.

dunes Hills or ridges of sand piled up by the wind.

equator The equator is an imaginary line around the middle of the earth.

floods Sudden gushes of water in a usually dry area of land. Floods can occur when heavy rainfall causes a river to overflow.

irrigation The way in which water is supplied to land in order to grow crops.

minerals Substances which are not alive and can be dug out of the ground. Copper and gold are minerals.

nomads People who travel from place to place in search of food, water and fresh grazing land for their animals.

oasis An area in a desert where water is on the surface.

reptiles Animals which have a scaly skin and which lay eggs, like snakes or lizards.

tribes Groups of people who share the same social customs and beliefs, and live together in the same area.

tropical Situated within an area near the equator, on either side of it.

Index

Photographic credits: Bruce
Coleman Ltd (M Fogden) 11,
(C Huges) 17, (Henneghein) 23,
(J R Brownlie) 29; Robert Harding
Picture Library 3, 25; Eric and
David Hosking 27; Hutchison
Library 19, 21, (D Brinicombe)
14; Frank Lane Picture Agency
(Silvestris) 7, (W Wisniewski) 9;
OSF (R Toms) 5.